10699318

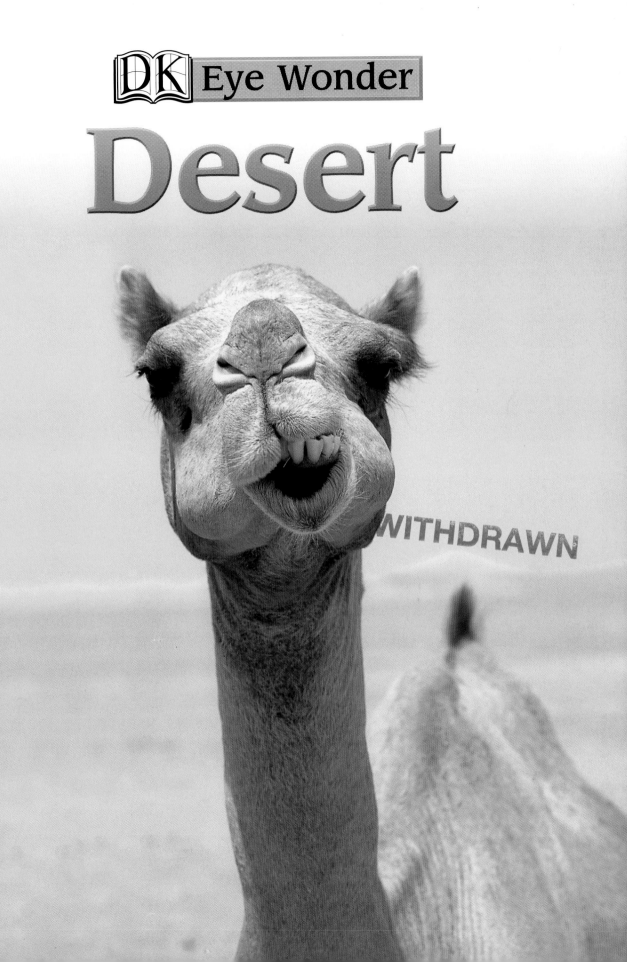

DK Eye Wonder

Desert

LONDON, NEW YORK,
MELBOURNE, MUNICH, and DELHI

Written and edited by Fleur Star
Designed by Clare Shedden

Publishing manager Susan Leonard
Managing art editor Rachael Foster
Picture researcher Liz Moore
Production Sarah Jenkins
DTP designer Ben Hung
Jacket designer Mary Sandberg

Consultant Dr. Kim Dennis-Bryan

Published in the United States in 2007 by
DK Publishing
375 Hudson Street, New York, NY 10014

A catalog record for this book
is available from the Library of Congress.

ISBN 978-0-7566-2908-3 (Hardcover)
ISBN 978-0-7566-2909-0 (ALB)

Color reproduction by Colourscan, Singapore
Printed and bound in Italy by L.E.G.O.

Discover more at
www.dk.com

Contents

What is a desert?

About one-fifth of the world is desert—arid (dry) land where less than 10 in (25 cm) of rain falls in a whole year. Most people think that deserts are hot, sandy, empty places—but is that true for every desert?

"Deserts are just a lot of sand."
Sandy deserts, such as the Sahara, may have huge sand dunes, but they are most made up of rocks and gravel. Many dese have oases or rivers flowing through the:

Cactus plants grow in American deserts, such as the Sonoran.

Camels easily cross the large dunes in the Sahara Desert.

"There's no life in the desert."

Compared to other parts of the world, such as forests, deserts are quite empty. But there are plants, animals, and even people living in deserts.

"It's hot in the desert."

Not always! Coastal deserts are cool, and cold deserts have freezing days during the winter. Even in hot deserts, where the sun beats down during the day, it gets very cold at night.

The Atacama Desert is cool because it is high up in the mountains.

5

Where in the world?

There are different ways of describing a desert, such as by temperature (is it hot or cold?) or where it is (is it on the coast?). Most deserts are near the tropics, where the weather is hot and dry.

Map key

● Hot deserts—these are very hot during the day, and any water here evaporates quickly.

● Cool coastal deserts—these deserts have cool air blowing in from the sea.

● Cold deserts—these have extremely cold winters, but they can still be very hot in the summer.

● Antarctic—this desert is unlike any other: it's frozen!

NORTH AMERICA

Great Basin

Tropic of Cancer   Mojave   Sonoran

Chihuahua

Equator

SOUTH AMERICA

Atacama

Tropic of Capricorn

Patagonia

Hot deserts are subtropical: they lie near the tropics of Cancer and Capricorn. This is the hottest part of the globe.

Coastal deserts are also subtropical, but they are not as warm as hot deserts because cold currents in the ocean keep the air cool.

ǝdoɹn

6

Cold deserts lie outside the tropics, farther away from the equator than hot deserts. A band of cold deserts stretches across central Asia.

at doesn't have a desert?

EUROPE

Kara Kum

Kyzyl Kum

Gobi

Takla Makan

Great Salt Desert

ASIA

MIDDLE EAST

Sahara

Thar

Arabian

AFRICA

Great Sandy

Tanami

Gibson

Simpson

Namib

Kalahari

Great Victoria

AUSTRALIA

ANTARCTICA

Antarctica is not like other deserts because it never gets hot. There's no water here because the snow does not melt.

Answer

7

Stacks of sand

Deserts are not entirely made up of sand—many of them are full of rocks and gravel, too. But there are still thousands of square miles (kilometers) of sand. So where did it all come from?

Elephant Rock is in the Mojave Desert.

Elephants rock!

As mountains wear away, they leave behind shapes called pinnacles. Many look like towers or needles, but others appear a arches or even animals.

Wind also creates sand, blowing across sandstone mountains and reducing them to dust.

From mighty mountains...

Most of the tiny grains of sand found in sandy deserts were once mountains! They were worn down by ice and water that covered the planet millions of years ago.

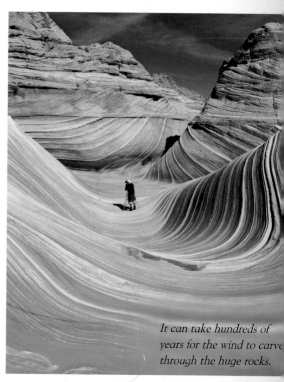

It can take hundreds of years for the wind to carve through the huge rocks.

Funny flowers

Desert roses are not real plants, but are made of crystals. When groundwater evaporates, it leaves behind crystals. These grow between grains of sand, creating "flowers."

Colorful carvings

These amazing rocks have been carved into shape by the wind. As the outer layers wear away, it reveals the colorful layers—or strata—of different types of rock that make up the mountains.

The world's highest dune is in the Gobi. It is around 1,640 ft (500 m) tall.

Dazzling dunes

Dunes are big hills of sand that are blown into shape by the wind. Plants or other obstacles block the sand and stop it from moving, so it piles up into a dune.

Dunes can form different shapes, depending on the direction the wind blows. This one, in the Namib Desert, is crescent shaped.

Dust storm!

A solid-looking wall of dust 1 mile (1.6 km) high is coming toward you. Suddenly the air is thick with swirling dust; it gets into your clothes and possessions, you can't see, and you can't breathe. Watch out, it's a dust storm!

Stranded

While robes and veils keep out the worst of the storm, dust still gets inside clothes. The only thing to do if caught outside in a storm is to huddle together and wait it out.

Saving face

Camels are too big to hide from a storm, but they can close their nostrils to stop sand from getting up their noses. A thin third eyelid brushes sand out of their eyes.

Long eyelashes stop most of the sand from getting into the eyes.

tormy city
eijing, in China, is more than
000 miles (1,600 km) from the
obi Desert. But six times a year,
obi dust turns the city's air yellow,
aking it difficult to breathe.

What are dust storms?
hey are strong winds that blow
uge gusts of dust for thousands
of miles (kilometers).
The dust is made
of sand that the
weather has worn
into fine grains.

You devil!
Dust devils are common in desert areas, where the land is flat and the air is still. In North America these whirling winds are called "dancing devils"; in Australia they are "willy willies."

SINGING DUNES
A Saharan legend tells the story of spirits, or *djenouns*, that sing from inside sand dunes. What really happens is that in the evening after a storm the wind causes sand grains to slip down the dune. The moving sand makes a deep groaning sound—the dune is singing!

Storms can be made up of both dust and sand.

The stronger the wind, the farther the dust will be blown.

Sand is too heavy to be blown far. It can be lifted 2 ft (50 cm) above ground.

Water of life

An oasis is a source of life in the dry desert. Plants grow where underground water is close to the surface; animals come to drink from the pools; and nomads move their homes to be near the water.

Water carrier

Sandgrouse really fill up at an oasis! They soak up wa[ter] in their breast feathers and then fly back to their nests so their chicks can drink it.

Dried dates

Dates are a staple food for people in the desert. There may be 1,000 dates in each huge bunch. Once dried, the fruit will never rot.

Date palms are typically found in North Africa and the Middle East.

Water fall

The water in an oasis comes from rainfall—but it might not have fallen here. Water can seep through porous rocks undergroun[d] and come to the surface where the ground is low.

Thirsty work

Sometimes water in a desert needs a little help in coming to the surface. These people from a village in the Sahara draw their water from a well they have dug.

Nile River, Africa

Going green

Some deserts have rivers running through them. The water is useful for irrigation, turning barren land into fertile farmland.

Safety in numbers

Many animals gather at oases, so it's wise to keep a look out for predators while drinking. This pair of gemsbok take turns to drink and stand guard.

Providing for the family

Twice a day, women in the Thar Desert, India, walk many miles (kilometers) to fill their pots with water. They carry the heavy loads home on their heads.

The Sahara

The world's biggest desert covers almost the entire north of Africa. The Sahara is a hot desert, which means it is hot during the day all year round: the temperature can reach 136 °F (58 °C) on a summer's day.

Seas of sand
During the Cretaceous period, around 65 million years ago, a huge sea covered the land where the Sahara is now. Today, the only "seas" in Africa are those made up of sand.

The Arabic word *sahra* gives the Sahara its name. It means "desert."

The real Sahara
Imagine a typical Sahara view: huge *ergs*, or sand dunes, as far as the eye can see... Actually, the Sahara is only 15 percent sand. Most of the rest is made up of gravel or rock, called *reg* and *hammada*.

ensible sunbathing

old-blooded rainbow lizards warm up in the orning sunshine, becoming bright blue and d as they get hotter. When the sun gets too rong, they shelter under rocks to keep from eing cooked.

Locust overload

There are more insects in the desert than any other animal. Just one swarm of locusts may contain millions of the plant-eating pests. They strip plants in minutes, leaving nothing for anything else to eat.

Find out about me on page 22!

Dromedary camels live in the Sahara, but they are not wild.

Staying alive

Deserts are dry places where water and food are in short supply. Animals out searching for food during the day also have to cope with the extreme heat in hot deserts. So how do the animals survive?

Who needs to drink?

A spadefoot toad can stay under ground for months. It wraps itself in a cocoon of dried skin and lives off the water stored in its bladder.

Food and drink

Many small antelopes, such as these springbok, graze on grasses and leaves. They get enough water to survive just from their food—but if given the chance they will also drink from pools.

When the feet on the ground get too hot, the lizard changes over

Cool moves

Shovel snouted lizards keep cool by dancing! They lift up their feet two at a time to keep from burning them on the hot desert floor.

We've got it licked
Red kangaroos lick their forearms to beat the heat: when the saliva evaporates, it cools them down. They can also smell out water and will travel 125 miles (200 km) to find water during drought.

Sidewinding snake species include some vipers and adders.

The snake curls up to make a loop, lifts the loop off the sand, and throws it forward to move along.

Making tracks
Sidewinder snakes don't slither forward, but travel sideways in an S-shape. This way, only part of the snake's belly comes into contact with the hot sand.

The tracks show where the snake lifts up and sets down.

Taking a dive
Sand skinks are also called sandfish because they "swim" through the sand. The sand is a little cooler just beneath the surface, and it's also a safe place to hide.

17

Night hunters

Even in hot deserts, temperatures plummet at night because there are no clouds in the sky to keep in the heat. Animals that find the daytime too hot come out at sunset, ready to find food.

Sharp eyes

Owls are expert nighttime hunters. Their large eyes allow lots of light to pass through, and they also have excellent hearing. Loose feathers on the owl's wings help it fly silently.

The cute-looking cat is really a sharp-clawed, big-toothed, fearsome predator.

Sand cats are about the same size as a small pet cat, but have much thicker fur.

Night facts

● Many animals that are nocturnal (active at night), such as foxes, have thick fur to keep them warm. During the day, the fur reflects the sun.

● Rodents are too small to be active in the daytime: they would overheat very quickly.

The viper bares its fangs and strikes at the sand cat in defense.

"Cat"-ch me if you can

Sand cats creep up close to their prey before making a sudden kill with their strong claws and teeth. If there's nothing on the surface to eat, the cat will dig under the ground.

orpions use
eir tails to
ect attackers
th venom.

Rodents are eaten by many predators, such as owls, cats, foxes, and snakes.

Little leaper

Jerboas are small rodents, but they take great leaps to escape predators! Bounding across the desert on its powerful hind legs, it races to get to its burrow before an owl grabs it.

I hear you

Hunting in the dark, fennec foxes use their senses of smell and hearing to find food such as insects, which is one reason why they have huge ears.

sting at both ends

orpions have needle-sharp tails
cked with venom, but they only
e their sting in defense. When
nting for food, such as geckos,
ey catch prey with their claws.

The agama must kill the scorpion quickly to avoid being stung.

unter becomes hunted

he desert agama is a diurnal
aytime) animal that eats small
nimals. Hunting prey that sleeps
ring the day makes catching it
at much easier!

Poison!

These creatures are among the deadliest in the desert. Whether they have eight legs or none at all, you had better watch your step to avoid them— they may use their venom for attack as well as defense.

Yellow scorpion

Arachnid facts

Scorpions and spiders are both arachnids, and they share a common way of finding food.

● Hunting at night, they feel for vibrations as prey approaches.

● They can feed only on liquids. Once they have killed their prey, they squirt digestive juices all over the victim, turning it into pulp.

Tarantula trap

Rather than spin webs, tarantulas ambu prey. Large tarantulas crush their prey w their huge fangs, but smaller ones kill by biting their victims and injecting venom.

The lizard's tail is its food store. It is full of fa similar to a camel's hum

Like all reptiles, the Gila monster has scaly skin. It also has strong legs for digging burrows.

It's a monster

There are just two species of venomous lizards, and the slow-moving, chunky Gila monster is one. It use its venom to kill small mammals, food that it finds by smell.

icing with death

red and yellow death adder lies
amouflaged on the Australian desert
oor. The snake waits for prey to cross
path—then makes a surprise strike.

Watching, waiting

The horned viper does not rely on just
camouflage. It buries itself in the sand,
with just its eyes and horns showing,
and lies in wait for its prey.

Snake, rattle, and roll

When a western diamondback
rattlesnake is threatened, it coils
up and shakes its rattle in defense.
But while the snake is venomous,
the rattle is actually harmless.

*The rattlesnake kills
by biting its victim and
injecting it with venom.*

*The rattle is made up
of a chain of scales that
make a noise when the
snake shakes its tail.*

Camels up close

There are two camel species, dromedary and bactrian, but 90 percent of the world's camels are dromedary. Known as "ships of the desert," camels can carry heavy loads over vast distances.

The camel's top lip is split so it can eat thorny plants.

Many dromedaries live in the Sahara

Extralong eyelashes protect the camel's eyes from sand.

Camel trains carry people, nomads' tents, or goods to sell at market.

Pale fur reflects the sunlight.

Bactrian brother

The bactrian has two humps and a thick winter coat that molts in the summer. Many domestic bactrians live in the Gobi Desert, but they are endangered in the wild.

...ot the hump

...dromedary has just the one hump,
...t it can weigh up to 30 lb (14 kg).
...contains fat, but when the camel
...es up this store of food, the hump
flops over to one side.

Thick fur keeps the camel warm at night, and protects against the sun in the day.

...t there are none left in the wild.

...camel spreads its weight ...to large, padded feet ...at don't sink into the ...nd when it walks.

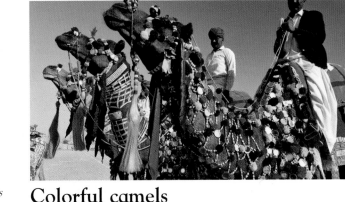

Colorful camels

People decorate their camels for the Desert Festival of Jaisalmer, in India. The animals are not merely transportation; they also provide milk and meat.

Filling station

Camels can go without drinking for more than a week, but when they reach a well or oasis, they can swallow 30 gallons (110 liters) in 10 minutes!

On your mark...

Camel racing is popular in Australia and Arabia. This traditional sport is now big business, with lots of money spent on preparing for races.

Down under

Australia

Nearly half of Australia is desert. The Gibson, Great Sandy, and Great Victoria together form the Outback. All the deserts are home to some very strange-looking animals!

The mole's tiny eyes are hidden—it uses smell and touch to find its way around.

Coming up for the kill

Marsupial moles live underground, only surfacing if they detect food. Their strong, flat claws are ideal fo burrowing—and for killing prey.

Kangaroos are marsupials—they carry their young in a pouch.

A red kang joey spends about 190 days in its mother's pouc It might return for anoth 35 days to sleep and feed or if danger threatens.

The very long, strong ta gives a kangaroo stabilit and power when it hops.

Mob rule

Millions of red kangaro live all over Australia, i groups (called "mobs") of up to 10 animals. Male kangaroos deliver powerful kicks from thei hind legs to show who's boss within the mob.

Honey hoarders

Honeypot ants are so full of food they cannot move. Other ants in the colony bring them food to keep them fat; then, when food is scarce, the colony feeds on the sugar that the "living pantries" vomit up.

spiky character

...e short-nosed echidna routs ...t ants and termites with ...snout, then licks them ...with its long, sticky tongue. ...s a monotreme—a mammal ...it lays eggs.

Spines provide water as well as defense: the lizard drinks dew that collects on them.

Get the point

Under all those spines is a lizard! The thorny devil needs such protection because the small reptile moves very slowly, seeking insects to eat. It can swallow 2,500 of them in one meal.

Bigger and bolder

Up to seven times bigger than a thorny devil, a sand monitor doesn't need spines. It uses its strong tail as a whip to strike attackers.

Cactus country

The cactus is the plant world's symbol of the desert. However, you won't find them in every desert—these spiky succulents only grow wild in American deserts, including the Sonoran, Mojave, and Chihuahua.

Gila woodpeckers brave the spines to make nesting holes inside the cacti. When they move out, elf owls move in!

Green giant

Giant saguaro cacti gr in the Sonoran Desert. They can reach 50 ft (15 m) tall and live for more than 200 years. Like all cacti, their stems a covered with spines, which are a kind of adapted leaf.

Spines give defence against animals that try to eat the water-filled cactus.

Cacti facts

- It takes around 75 years for a saguaro to grow an "arm."

- Cacti lose less water through their spines than they would if they had normal leaves.

- Two-thirds of the weight of a giant saguaro is water. That's enough to fill 1,000 bathtubs.

Spiky sunscreen

The "old man cactus" has more than spikes on its stem: it has hairs, too, which act as a screen against the strong desert sun. White spines are especially good for reflecting the sunlight.

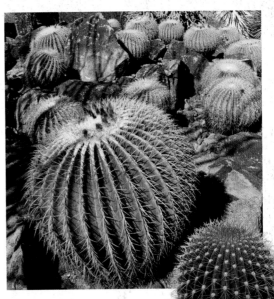

People use aloe juice in cosmetics and as an ointment for cooling burns.

Aloe aloe

Succulents are plants that store water in their stem or leaves. Like this aloe, they also have a waxy coating to protect the leaves from the sun and wind.

Full to bursting

A cactus is a giant water tank. The plant draws in water through its roots and stores so much that its stem grows fat. The creases on the stem expand just like an accordion.

Prickly pears also grow in Australia. They were brought there 200 years ago.

This fruit tastes sharp!

The big, flat pads of a prickly pear are not leaves, but stems. The pads and fruit are covered in spines—but that doesn't stop animals from eating them!

The desert in bloom

All plants need water to survive, but it can be hard to find water in the desert—and to keep from losing it. Desert plants have developed clever ways of finding and storing water in the driest of lands.

Acacias have thorns to stop animals from grazing on their juicy leaves.

Pebble plants blend in with desert gravel, hidden from animals that might eat them.

The root of the matter

Acacia trees provide shade and shelter for many animals in the open desert. The trees can grow in the dry land because they have very long roots that search for moisture deep underground.

The ends of the leaves may dry out and die, but they keep on growing—up to 20 ft (6 m) long!

It takes two

Plants lose water through their leaves, so the best way to keep water is to have few leaves. Welwitschia and pebble plants have just two each, although they could hardly look more different.

*Roses of Jericho
are also called
"resurrection plants."*

ack to life
When there is no water,
se of Jericho plants dry
so much they look like
ey are dead. But a "miracle"
ccurs when the rains come:
e plant comes back to life!

Water storage tanks
The fruit of a desert melon plant is full of
stored water. Thirsty animals wandering
through the desert devour whole patches
of these wild plants.

*The Sonoran looks
empty in the dry season.*

Speedy bloomers
The Sonoran Desert becomes
a riot of color after a spring
rainfall. Seeds that fell on the
dry ground the year before
quickly germinate and grow
into flowers in just a few weeks.

Who lives there?

Despite the blistering daytime heat, freezing cold nights, and dusty, dry environment, there are people living in every hot desert in the world. Many of them are nomadic: they move around the desert in search of water.

Unlike Bedouins, Aborigines keep cool by not wearing many clothes.

Less is more

Aborigines in the Australian deserts traditionally wo[re] very little. Now they mostly wear modern dress, but will put on loincloths and body paint for ceremonies.

Bedouins wear long, flowing robes and head scarves to keep the sun off them.

Bedouin men play the rabbaba to entertain guests.

Bedouins and Tuaregs used to load their tents and possessions onto camels when moving home. Today, they often use trucks.

Mobile homes

The Bedouins of the Middle East are nomads, so they need houses that are easy to transport and put up. Their rug-lined tents have dark covers made of goat hair, keeping the inside cool and shady.

Houses ar[e]

Tuaregs live in the Sahara.

Desert dwellings: Permanent...

People living in the Thar Desert are not nomadic. They build solid homes out of local materials: straw, sand, and camel dung.

Temporary...

In the Kalahari, San people shelter in grass huts when the rains come. In the summer they might not build huts at all, just a screen to block out the wind.

Underground!

Whole towns of stone- or brick-built houses can be found in some deserts. In Australia, opal miners carved houses out of cool underground caves.

People of the veil

A Tuareg man is easily recognized by his veil, the *tagelmust*. Tuaregs believe that the veil protects against evil spirits. It also shields the face from sand.

Clothes need to keep people warm at night, but cool during the day.

There isn't much furniture to pack up when moving.

A curtain separates the women's area from the men's, giving them privacy.

Desert daily life

There are many things that people do every day, such as working, making meals, and playing sports or music. People in the desert do all this, too—but probably not in the same way as you!

The arrow is coated with poison that comes from beetle larvae.

Hunting is the main way San find food.

Arts and crafts

Making jewelry is one of many desert crafts. Women work with leather, wool, and beads, while men forge metal into jewelry, saddle decorations, and swords.

Going hunting

It takes a lot of skill to hunt in the desert. San men know how to follow animal tracks to find prey such as antelope. Silently they crouch low, take aim, and kill the animal with their poison arrows.

Aborigines used boomerangs as their hunting weapons, throwing the curved wooden clubs at prey.

The speediest racing camels have long, straight legs and big muscles, but small feet.

Local races are a way of reviving old traditions as people in the desert become more modern.

Women spin the wool and dye it with bright colors.

A woman's work

While the men are out working, Bedouin women run the home, doing everything from milking the camels and cooking, to making clothes and getting firewood.

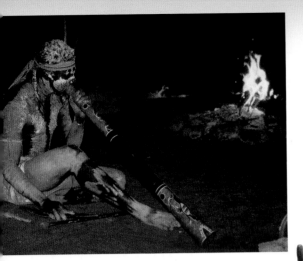

The wool comes from the family's goats and sheep, or may be bought.

ime to relax

aying music is a popular astime in the long, dark desert enings. Aborigines traditionally ay a didgeridoo, a hollow tree anch that is as tall as a child!

Clothes, bags, and rugs are woven from sheep's wool.

Who's the best?

Camels are such a major part of desert people's lives, they are even used for sport. Traditional camel racing gave people the chance to show off how good their camel was.

Food and drink

It can be a daily struggle to find enough to eat and drink in the desert. Nomads can't run to the supermarket to fill up a freezer with food; they can't even turn on a faucet for water. So from where do they get their food and drink?

The witchetty grub, a kind of moth larva, is the best known "bush tucker"—food that Aborigines find in the desert.

Millet grain is pounded and mad[e] into porridge.

Fresh food

Tuaregs eat what their anima[ls] give them: meat, eggs, and dai[ry] products such as milk and yogu[rt]. They sell any extra food to bu[y] millet from local markets.

People decorate their eggshells to show whose is whose.

Egg stores

Water is such a precious resource that it needs to be stored carefully. San people fill empty ostrich eggshells with water and bury them to keep them cool and safe.

ood for all

edouin men share their meals
th guests, scooping up rice and
eat with their fingers from a large
nter plate. Women cook the
eal, then go to eat
their own part
the tent.

*Plenty of food
can fit onto this
plate: it can hold a
whole cooked sheep!*

*is very important to be a
generous host: one day you might need a return meal.*

Time for tea

Tuaregs show hospitality
through their tea ceremony.
Green tea leaves, sugar, and
water are boiled on an open
fire to make a strong
brew for the guests.

*Bedouins prefer
coffee to tea and
serve three small
cups to each guest.*

*It's a man's job to
greet guests and
perform the tea
ceremony.*

*The pot is
poured from
high up so the
tea is frothy.*

Twice as tough

Animals and plants in cold deserts, such as the Gobi and Patagonia, don't just have to cope with hot summers—they also have to survive freezing winters, when the temperature can plummet to -40 °F (-40 °C).

There aren't many plants in the rocky Gobi, but the saxaul grows here in clumps. The woody shrub grows twice as tall as a person.

Leopard geckos sear for food at night, storing fat in the tails to get by in extreme weather. In winter, they hibernat

A coat for all seasons

Bactrian camels have woolly coats to keep warm in the winter, but in the summer the heat can be overbearing. So in the spring, they begin their annual molt.

BACK FROM THE BRINK?

Przewalski horses used to roam the Gobi, but today they are officially extinct in the wild. Luckily, some survived in zoos, and these were used in a breeding program so the species could be brought back to the Gobi. Now there are around 1,500 horses in Gobi national parks.

Welcome home

It's hard to find food in the snowy Gobi winter.

The hair falls off in thick clumps, leaving a sparse layer for the summer. It will grow back in the fal

Changing with the weather
Hairy armadillos change their behavior with the seasons. In the winter, when it is cold, they are active in the daytime; but in the summer they stay in burrows to avoid the heat, and come out at night instead.

What am I?
The mara looks a bit like a large rabbit or a small deer, but it is actually a rodent, so it is closer to being a huge rat! Maras can run very fast, up to 30 mph (48 km/h), when escaping predators in the open

Even in the summer, strong winds keep the Patagonia Desert bare.

Patagonia, in South America, lies in the shadow of the Andes Mountains. Very few plants can survive the dry weather and strong winds here.

A long walk home
Magellanic penguins live on the coast and feed in the sea. But in the breeding season they waddle 1 mile (1.6 km) inland across the desert dunes, where they dig burrows to lay their eggs in.

Living in the Gobi

Mongolian nomads move around to find pasture for their animals. It's not easy in the extreme Gobi weather—the nomads have to settle before the snow does.

Dried animal dung is collected, piled up, and burned as fuel.

The nomads wear thick, warm clothes in the winter.

Hunting
Golden eagles are important to the Mongolians. The men train the birds to hunt for foxes and rabbits.

Follow the herd
Mongolians are herders: they keep camels, yaks, sheep, and goats for milk, meat, and wool. Nothing goes to waste—even the dung is used!

Gers in the Gobi
Mongolians live in *gers*, sturdy mobile homes that can keep out the cold weather. The *ger's* wooden frame collapses and fits neatly onto a truck when it's time to move on.

A hole in the ceiling acts as a chimney and a window to let in light.

A sloping roof keeps the snow off in winter.

tarting young

Mongolians are most famous for being
orsemen. They have a saying that children
re taught to ride before they can walk!
Horses are also milked as well as ridden.

Sports skills

Mongolian men work hard and play
hard. Their favorite sport is wrestling.
Along with horsemanship and archery,
it is one of their "three manly skills."

*It's the women's job
to milk the animals.
Fermented horse milk
makes a tasty drink.*

Interior design

Inside the home is warm and snug.
While the practical *ger* looks plain from
the outside, lots of bright colors inside
cheer up the bleak landscape.

Not all gers *are
entirely traditional—
some even have TVs.*

*The heavy felt walls are
made from sheep's wool.
The ropes are yak hair.*

39

It's cool to be coastal

The Atacama Desert in South America runs alongside the Pacific Ocean, yet it is the driest place on Earth. Some parts of the cool desert have not seen rainfall since records began—that's at least 400 years.

WHY IS THE ATACAMA SO DRY?

Even compared to other deserts, the Atacama is extra dry. When the sun has warmed the air in the desert, no rain falls because warm air holds in water. There is fog from the ocean to the west, but it is quickly burnt off by the sun. And to the east the Andes Mountains block any rainclouds, which leaves the Atacama trapped high and dry in the middle.

Watch this space

The Atacama landscape is so bare, it has been compared to the Moon and Mars—so much so that NASA uses it to test space equipment.

Coastal cacti

The fog that forms over the ocean provides just enough moisture for plants such as cacti to grow along the coast. Farther inland, the desert is too dry for any plants to grow at all.

As well as being coastal, the Atacama is high up in the Andes Mountains, where the air is cool.

Cold ocean currents keep the air temperature cool.

The same difference

Although still very dry, the Namib Desert in southwest Africa is different from the Atacama because it is not mountainous. Fog rolls in from the sea over vast sand dunes, bringing water to animals, including fog-basking beetles.

As moisture condenses on the beetle's shell, the insect bends forward to roll the droplet into its mouth to drink.

Camel cousins

Guanacos are the South American relatives of camels. They can wander through the desert for many days without needing to drink.

Guanacos pick up moisture through their food as they graze on the Andean slopes.

Flamingo frenzy

There is some water in the Atacama, mostly in salt lakes. These lakes are home to thousands of flamingos, which gather to feed in the shallow waters.

41

Is it a desert?

Antarctica, the continent around the South Pole, has very little precipitation (what scientists call rain, snow, and hail). This makes it a desert— and it's the biggest in the world.

Whiteout!

There's no rain at all in the world's coldest, windiest continent—it's so cold, it gets snow instead. Not much actually falls, but strong winds blow snow around, causing blinding blizza

Plentiful penguins

Emperor penguins only go on land to raise their chicks. After laying her egg, the female returns to the ocean for food, leaving the male in charge.

The only large animals in Antarctic

Left on his own, the male doesn't eat while he looks after the egg.

Eight weeks later, the females return with food for their newborn chicks.

Where are all the plants?
Mosses and algae are the only plants in Antarctica. There are no trees or bushes; their roots would not be able to get through the frozen ground.

Like mosses and algae, types of fungus called lichen grow on rocks in the Antarctic.

The wrong name?
What do crabeater seals eat mostly? Not crabs, but krill! As they swim in the sea, they lock their teeth together into a "sieve" to collect the food from the water.

Krill are shrimplike animals.

...ve in the sea. There's not enough food for them to live on land.

What about the Arctic?
The area around the North Pole, where polar bears live, is an icecap on top of the sea. Although the Arctic has no rain, it also has no land, so it can't be called a desert.

The growing desert

The amount of desert in the world is getting larger. Rivers are drying up, grasslands are disappearing, and more and more land is turning bare. There are two main reasons for desertification: nature and human beings.

Do you use energy-saving lightbulbs and recycled paper?

What's the problem?

It's thought that 250 million people will be affected by desertification. The growing desert will bury homes and make it hard to find food, and dust storms will reach big cities more often, triggering diseases such as asthma.

Desertification facts

Most scientists agree that the main reason that deserts are spreading is land misuse. This includes:

- chopping down trees
- clearing land for farming
- overgrazing animals

More than a quarter of land on Earth is at risk of desertification.

Sahel survivors

Ostriches can be found in the Sahel, the semidesert south of the Sahara. Not many other animals can survive there; they move away or die out as the Sahel's desert conditions get worse.

Flightless ostriches walk long distances to find grass and other plants to eat.

The grass holds down the sand, stopping it from blowing away.

Sand fences

One way to stop the desert form spreading is to plant trees to hold back the sand. In China, people have planted grass in the Gobi to stop the sand and dust storms from reaching the cities so often.

The crops are watered by a pipe that turns in the middle of the circle.

Crop circles

These huge green circles found in American, African, and Middle Eastern deserts are fields! Irrigating, or watering, the land allows farmers to grow crops such as wheat and tomatoes.

Greedy goats

People in the desert keep goats because they provide wool, milk, and meat. But goats are not good for the desert—they eat everything, stripping the land of plants. The bare soil gets blown away, leaving just sand behind.

Goats have been introduced to many deserts in Africa and India.

Glossary

Here are the meanings of some words it is useful
to know when learning about deserts.

Arachnid animals that have eight legs and bodies divided into two sections, such as spiders and scorpions.

Arid when something is arid, it is very dry. Arid land has very little water.

Barren something that is empty of life. Barren land cannot support plants.

Camouflage a color or pattern that blends in with its surroundings, so it can't be seen.

Cold-blooded animals that warm up or cool down depending on the temperature around them. Reptiles are cold-blooded.

Desert an area that gets less than 10 in (25 cm) of rainfall in a year. In a desert, more water evaporates than falls.

Desertification the spread of desertlike conditions.

Diurnal animals that are diurnal are active during the day.

Dune a hill of sand that has been blown into shape by the wind.

Dust storm strong winds that pick up sand and dust. Dust can be blown thousands of miles (kilometers).

Fertile when an animal or plant can reproduce, it is fertile. Ground that is fertile is good for growing plants.

Global warming the rise in the Earth's temperature. It affects the world's weather, causing droughts and severe storms.

rigation watering the land sing man-made methods ch as pipes or canals. Desert rmers use irrigation to water eir crops.

Mammal animals that produce ilk to feed their young, such as mels, cats, and humans.

Marsupial mammals whose males carry their young in pouch, such as kangaroos.

octurnal animals that are octurnal are active during e night.

omad a person that regularly oves from place to place, king their home with them.

Oasis a fertile area within a desert. Oases usually have a pool of water surrounded by trees. Animals come to drink the water.

Pinnacle the remains of a mountain or large rock that has been worn away by the wind. They are often needle-shaped.

Predator an animal that hunts, kills, and eats other animals.

Prey the animal that is hunted, killed, and eaten by a predator.

Reptile animals that have tough, scaly skin, such as lizards and snakes. Most lay eggs rather than give birth to live young.

Rodent mammals that have strong front teeth for gnawing, such as jerboas.

Succulent plants that store water in their leaves or stem, such as cacti.

Venom a poisonous liquid. Snakes and scorpions have venom; they bite or sting to inject the venom as defense or for killing prey.

Warm-blooded the opposite of "cold-blooded." Animals and birds that can keep their body temperatures on a constant level. Mammals are warm-blooded.

Index

Acknowledgments

Dorling Kindersley would like to thank:
Andy Cooke for artwork; Simon Mumford for cartography.

Picture credits

The publisher would like to thank the following for their kind permission to reproduce their photographs:
(a=above; c=center; b=below; l=left; r=right; t=top)
Alamy Images: Arco Images 39cl, 39tl; Around the World in a Viewfinder 32tr; Suzy Bennett 34tl; Blickwinkel 12-13bc, 19tc, 24cr; Danita Delimont 38tl; Dinodia Images 23tr; Elvele Images/CGE 42bl, 43br; Robert Estall Photo Agency 31tl; Mark Eveleigh 25bc; Pavel Filatov 39crb; Glen Islet 27tr; Israel images 6bl; Andrea Jones 27tl; Juniors Bildarchiv 46bl; Wolfgang Kaehler 39tr; Tomas Kaspar 8br; David Kilpatrick 12ca; Emmanuel Lattes 27br; Lou Linwei 11tl; LOOK Die Bildagentur der Fotografen GmbH 1c, 15br; Alex Maddox 25cra; Ellen McKnight 3br; Bernd Mellmann 14-15b; nagelestock.com 30t; Joe Nebrasz 43tr; Peter Richard Noble 31tr; Dale O'Dell 4-5c; Gerry Pearce 25bc; Peter Adams Photography 39bc; Picpics 8tr; Robert Preston 13br; Robert Harding Picture Library 23br, 35tr; Slick Shoots 46-47cb; Simon Stirrup 28tr; Stockfolio 22cl; David Tipling 43tl; Tribaleye Images/Jamie Marshall 4-5b; David Wall 31crb; Marcus Wilson-Smith 7tr; **Ardea:** John Cancalosi 2tl, 16cra; Jean-Paul Ferrero 24bc;

Mike W Gillam 24tr; François Grohier 37tl, 37tr; **John Conley:** John Conley 40tr; **Corbis:** Theo Allofs/Zefa 41b; Yann Arthus-Bertrand 14tr, 45cl, 45r; Craig Aurness 10bl, 10-11bc; Jonathan Blair 13tr; Fridmar Damm 2-3; Eyal Ofer 32-33b; Michael & Patricia Fogden 21tl; Gallo Images 6br, 34bl; George H H Huey 29c; Peter Johnson 28bc, 32cla, 32tl, 34br; Frans Lemmens 15tr, 48; David Muench 26c; Kazuyoshi Nomachi 8cl; Reuters 44tl, 45tl; Galen Rowell 42tr; Scott T. Smith 29crb; Sygma/Patrick Robert 15cr; Penny Tweedie 25tr; Steffan Widstrand 28ca; Alison Wright 13clb; **Eye Ubiquitous:** Hutchison 31cra; **FLPA:** Jim Brandenburg/Minden 41tl; Flip de Nooyer/Foto Natura 37b; Michael & Patricia Fogden 16bc, 41cl; Tom and Pam Gardner 17tl; Chris Mattison 21tr; Mark Moffett/Minden 20cra; Norbert Wu/Minden 42-43c; **Getty Images:** Robert Harding World Imagery 30bl; G K & Vicky Hart 22c; Michael Melford 11tr; George H. H. Huey Photography 27bl; **Impact Photos:** 30-31b; **Lonely Planet Images:** Graham Taylor 38bc; **Magnum Photos:** Steve McCurry 10tr; **naturepl.com:** Graham Hatherley 19cr; Tom Mangelsen 18tr; Vincent Munier 44b; Gabriel Rojo 41cr; **OSF:** 36br; John Brown 40b; Michael Fogden 17cr; Travel Library Ltd 4-5t; Ariadne van Zandbergen 35b; **Photolibrary:** Workbook Inc. 36tr; **Photoshot/NHPA:** Martin Harvey 29tr; Daniel Heuclin 17bl, 19bc, 19tl, 21b, 29tl; **PunchStock:** Goodshot 23cr; **Science Photo Library:** G K Lorenx 26ca; **stevebloom.com:** 7br; **Still Pictures:** 34tr; Joffe Dragesco 18cb; Raimund Franken 33tl; Thomas Haertrich 8-9, Hartmut Schwarzbach 30cr; **SuperStock:** age fotostock 15tl, 36bl; **Dr Olga Pereladova/WWF International:** 36tl

All other images © Dorling Kindersley.
For further information see www.dkimages.com